46

Sharp

Points

for well-rounded talks

by
Don Sharp

11593 Peacock
Indianapolis Ind
46236

A Division of Standard Publishing
Cincinnati, Ohio
40-038

Library of Congress Catalog Card No. 75-38224
ISBN: 0-87239-092-6

To Ruth,
a committed Christian and wife,
who shares in the highs and lows
of a minister's life

Acknowledgments

To all those people, so wise and not so wise, so committed and not so committed, who contributed so much, knowingly and unknowingly, to the writing of this book; especially those who encouraged me to finish what was started. My special thanks to those who typed and corrected manuscripts: Miss Janet Schultz, Dr. Eleanor Daniel, Mrs. Oka Negley, and Mrs. Barbara Johns.

54492

Contents

Warming Stations

Is not my word like as a fire? saith the Lord.
—Jeremiah 23:29

Entering the back door of the church recently, I was rather surprised to find three children standing just inside. There was a momentary silence, and then the eldest explained, "We came into the church to get warm."

It was chilly outside, all right. The mercury had dropped to a frigid -1, and the windchill factor drove the cold right through you. How glad I was that these children recognized the church building as a refuge from the biting cold.

Churches should be warming stations, places of refuge, along life's way. There, all people, rich or poor, black or white, male or female, could come in out of the cold of culture's biases and pride's hatefulness. If ever there were a place for generating warmth for the little people of the world, it ought to be Christ's church!

God's Word is light, but when it is preached and taught there is more than light. There is warmth. "Is not my word like fire?" said Jehovah. A warmth of God's love is reflected in His people as they relate to all people. For so long we have boasted ourselves as being people of the light, but fire is more than light; it is warmth. "God is love," wrote John. Let us, dear brothers, be more than reflections of light. Let us be known as reflections of God's love and light.

When people come in from the chill of the world, will they find God's Word like fire, or will it be phosphorescent—cold light without heat? God forbid! Let God's Word be a furnace bright and warm. Let us love one another as He first loved us.

Parable of the Sunflowers

Consider the lilies of the field. —Matthew 6:28

It has been interesting to watch the growth of sunflowers in a church neighbor's backyard. Sunflowers grow quickly and ever so large. They remind me of those big, yellow, smiling faces that were so popular a few years ago.

But today the sunflower heads were bowed as though each had come to a sacred place and were standing on holy ground. I couldn't help feeling that I should stop and bow my head too. Then it occurred to me that those bowing sunflowers weren't praying people, so I passed on to my car to go home to lunch. The pause in pace, however, did cause me to think: If I had it to do over again, that is, if I were just starting as a minister, I'd spend more time *praying* and less time worrying. I'd spend more time *being* than doing, and I'd spend more time *trusting* and less time doubting.

One might call this thing I've learned "The Lesson of the Sunflowers." All the time I have watched those flowers grow, I never once saw them show any signs of doubting the purpose of their existence. They never lost sight of what they were. Neither did they worry one minute over the lack of what was needed. They went on, day after day, just content to be what God created them to be— sunflowers.

Clogged-up Channels

Create in me a clean heart, O God; and renew a right spirit within me. —Psalm 51:10

It was a real mystery to try to figure out why the baptistery had gone cold. We went over our checklist several times: Is the pump turned on? Is the heater burner going? Is the water level correct? Are all the valves open? After doing this several times, with the proper waiting times between, and still cold water, we decided to consult a plumber.

The pipe fitters were not long in tracking down the problem. It was a bad case of "hardening of the arteries." The pipes, which were supposed to carry the hot water to the baptistery, were all clogged up. Mineral deposits had built up, layer upon layer, until there was no opening large enough for even a beam of light to penetrate. No wonder the baptistery had gone cold!

This might be a modern parable, illustrating what happens when the channels circulating light and love between God and man get all clogged up. The Christian goes cold.

What are the channels? An important incoming channel surely must be called "study" and an outgoing channel certainly must be "prayer." The thing that stops the warmth of God's love and light from coming and going is a buildup of many little things which accumulate. What things? Things like a little neglect, a little procrastination, a little passing doubt, a little disassociation here and a little shirking there. One keeps hanging onto the other, each adding on, until the value of study is obscure and the efficacy of prayer is questioned. These eventually stop the flow and human hearts turn hard and cold. Before long, men become dubious about the value or power of study and prayer, and then they quit studying and praying! The habits become set and the channels are closed. How can God's warmth get through pipes clogged up with neglect, procrastination, doubt, disassociation, and shirking? The truth of the matter is, it can't!

The plumbers solved the cold baptistery problem by pulling out the old clogged-up pipes and installing new ones. Maybe that's what some cold Christians ought to do—pull out those old "study and prayer habits" and put in some new ones. Then they would be open to all of God's wonderful, warming power!

For Women to Ponder

Instead of sweet smell there shall be stink; . . . and burning instead of beauty. —Isaiah 3:24

Manufacturers of a cigarette for women employ some shrewd advertising techniques to attract the market.

First, the cigarette was designed to be more slim than the regular cigarette, to appeal to all those women who are slim, imagine themselves slim, or wistfully wish they were slim. Puffing on a slim weed can be very symbolic.

Second, the name "Virginia" suggests superior quality, that of being pure, beautiful, and feminine. Virginia is one name that no one has ever given, or would ever give, to a male. Also, there is no state more beautiful than Virginia.

As a final grab for business, the clever ad writer for the "woman's cigarette" appeals to all the "libbers" with that notorious phrase, "You've come a long way, baby!" With that little jewel they have shown the girls how degrading it was, back in the "old days," when it was thought improper, unfeminine, and grossly ill-mannered for a lady to look like a smokestack and smell like a camel.

Well, things do change, and the girls *have* come a long way, as far as being able to smoke without being thought of as unfeminine. But it's such a dubious arrival, this "long way." The girls have come a long way, but to where?

Let us look at some destinations, or results. They have come to a shorter life expectancy, certainly. With every cigarette, one's life is shortened by the same amount of time it takes to smoke it. This may not be true of a "Virginia Slim." It is thinner, and thus has less tobacco. But the shorter life may have an equalizing effect on society, since women live longer than men. It looks as though the women, rather than the meek, will inherit the earth.

Another factor that casts doubt on the smoking woman's "arrival" is the effect that smoking has on newborn babies. Not only do the smokers have smaller babies; the little ones are also programmed during their impressionable years to rely upon external crutches to "calm one's nerves." They are not taught, at least by example, to look within for strength to meet and solve life's problems.

Yes, Ma'am, you've "come a long way, baby," since those "old days." You have won the "right" to smoke, smell, and die like a man. Somehow I fail to see these things as "coming a long way" toward anything particularly desirable. I'm just a male chauvinist who would like to see girls truly pure, truly beautiful, and truly feminine. Somehow a cigarette-smoking girl shatters that image for me. Do I expect too much of the mothers-to-be of the race? Perhaps, but I'm an incurable optimist. I figure if one may read and heed this little homily somewhere, someone may later thank me for a better-smelling wife, or maybe even a longer life.

What Is a Minister?

How shall they hear without a preacher? –Romans 10:14

A schoolteacher friend recently brought me some essays written by her third-graders in response to the question, "What is a minister?" The purpose, of course, was an exercise in creative writing. The results were sometimes controversial, oftentimes enlightening, and most of the time delightful.

The controversial concepts appeared when one little girl wrote, "A minister is a man that is higher than a priest. He works like a priest." Another eight-year-old had an altogther different idea: "A minister is a person in church who reads the sckerpt (Scripture). A minister is *not* as important as a priest." What puzzled me was that the first writer had the Italian name.

One essay that shook me in particular was the one that said, "When you go to church you see a man in front. He does most of the talking." I couldn't help wondering if I had left that same impression with a lot of people. My spirit was revived, however, with another little girl's comments, which may explain, if not justify, all that talking by the "man in front." She wrote, "A minister is a man that teaches people about God and Jesus. A minister helps people pray. A minister helps you live with Christ."

Some were more interested in what the minister wore than what he was. One little boy observed, "A minister wears a black cape with a little white thing around his neck."

Some minister somewhere surely had impressed one little boy with his importance, for he wrote, "He is a sertened (certain) kind of god." Wow! One must wonder what takes place in that church on any given Sunday. I was somewhat relieved to note that the boy had spelled "god" with a lowercase "g." Perhaps the writer was saying something profound with tongue in cheek.

As a minister, I was encouraged to read one little boy's observation, "A minister is a good person. They love people." Another, obviously having observed an important function of any preacher worth his salt, wrote, "A minister gets people together." But when all were read, the one that really lingered in my heart was the terse comment of the nine-year-old who said, "A minister helps clean people up."

Bring Jesus Home!

If any provide not for his own, and specially for those of his own house, he hath denied the faith, and is worse than an infidel.
                                                    −1 Timothy 5:8

Some years ago, I was in my study while several young married adults were practicing a play in the sanctuary. The telephone rang. Answering it, I recognized the voice of a child whose parents were in the play. He wanted to talk with his mother. When his mother answered the phone, I couldn't help overhearing her side of the conversation. She assured the boy, only as mothers can, that they would be home soon, and that it would be all right for the baby-sitter to pop some corn.

Answering some questions about what they were doing at the church, the mother explained that they were in a play, and that Daddy was playing the part of Jesus. Noting some discomfort in the mother's voice, I looked to see a question on her face as she held the now lifeless phone in her hand.

"What's the matter?" I asked.

"Well," she answered, "Kevin must have misunderstood me when I told him that his daddy was playing the part of Jesus. He said, 'Oh, goody! Tell Daddy to bring Jesus home with him!' and then hung up."

I couldn't help but wonder if that child had expressed a secret longing for daddies and mothers to do more than go to church, such as maybe bringing the Lord home with them.

When parents bring Jesus home with them, some spectacular things happen! The husband and wife will take time for love and companionship. Because of the example of the Lord, they will keep adding fuel to the fire of love by words and acts of appreciation for each other. Because of the forgiveness of Christ, when there is a misunderstanding the Christian couple will be quick to forgive and ask forgiveness. By entertaining the Lord in the home, the couple will avoid the home-wrecking habits of impatience, worry, nagging, jealousy, and all other forms of self-love. Knowing that God cares for the fall of the sparrow, the Christian couple will have a more secure attitude toward money, and will not worry over the future. Instead, he and she will face all hardships with faith in God and each other.

As the children grow up, they will have before them an example of what a good marriage is. Each is more likely to have a good marriage himself, as a result. Having had the security of a Christian home, he in turn is likely to bring Jesus home with him.

It is a very good idea: "Tell Daddy to bring Jesus home with him!"

Changelessness Amid Change

Jesus Christ the same yesterday, and to day, and for ever. —Hebrews 13:8

On a recent vacation, I returned to a farm in West Virginia where as a boy I roamed the woods, laid in new-mown grass, and climbed the apple trees. As my wife and I walked back to the edge of a woodland, to me it looked very much like I had remembered it. I pointed out a ledge and remembered that there used to be a huckleberry bush right under that ledge. As I climbed down, there it was, the berries just as ripe and luscious as they had been thirty-five years before. I picked a handful for my wife, and then we walked back over the fields through the orchard to the house. About the only thing that had changed was that the path had given way to a bath.

For a whole year I have been basking in the warmth of that experience. It was good to return to the place of my origin, but the fantastic truth was in noting what little change had taken place in a world so subjected to ripping out the old and pushing in the new.

I'm not opposed to progress. A bath is to be desired over a path any old time. I am wondering, though, how much change the human heart can endure. Must there not be some pilings deeply driven to hold onto when changes come? There's not much anyone can do to thwart the technological, sociological, and cultural changes, but with faith in a changeless Savior and confidence in a changeless Word, we can find the stability to give direction to all those changes.

The thing that has unnerved us so in the past years is not the technological, cultural, and sociological changes taking place; it is rather our having lost hold of the changeless God and the changeless Word to the extent that we are swept with the current into a great swirling whirlpool of physical, psychological, and spiritual uncertainty.

But look at this: "Jesus Christ is the same yesterday, today, and forever!" A good place to begin, therefore, in seeing things in true perspective is to take a walk through the changeless Word with the changeless Christ. Instead of being so frightened of the future, we might find the strength to make sure that all that is labeled "progress" really is.

Some reading this may have wandered away from life's only certainties: God and His Word. Why don't you come back? You had the certainty of an unchanging Lord; you can have that certainty again. Besides, the future needs the certainty of some people who are strong enough to give direction to change.

Managing Unmanageables

Resist the devil, and he will flee from you.   —James 4:7

During the depression, the big Hagenback-Wallace Circus came to our town, and Clyde Beatty was a featured attraction. Ever since I was a boy, I have had a yearning to see Clyde Beatty perform in the circus with his wild animals. There just weren't enough shekels in the family budget for us to go. As close as any of us children got was watching the big tents go up. I remember hearing the lions roar, but all I could do was imagine what it would be like to see Clyde Beatty putting those big cats through their paces.

When times were a little more affluent, I remember the big top was scheduled to return to our town again. As it happened, however, the day the show was supposed to begin, a big storm blew down the tents, and those superstitious circus people never again returned to our town. Just recently, though, I noticed that the Clyde Beatty Circus was going to be in a nearby city. I began breaking out all over with those boyhood goosebumps about finally getting to see old Clyde, whip and chair in hand, putting all those snarling jungle beasts in their places. Alas, this time it was sickness that kept me from the big arena. Perhaps another day, another place—

Anyway, it started me thinking. Maybe old Clyde Beatty's mastery of those jungle cats is pretty tame stuff compared with that big cat we Christians have to face every day in the arena of life. Mind you, I'm not ready to get in a cage with twenty jungle creatures of any description; but there's hardly a day goes by that most of us do not face some pretty dangerous situations, due to the fact that the devil, "as a roaring lion, walketh about, seeking whom he may devour" (1 Peter 5:8). Now, there's one cat that would like to put us down for keeps, but I have some good news from an old lion tamer. If you resist the devil, he's bound to split out and head for safer places. In his letter, James said, "Resist the devil, and he will flee from you" (4:7).

The problem so many Christians are having is that they aren't resisting! the devil snarls, and the fainthearted tremble. He roars, and the fearful run. We have to stand fast and resist Satan, steadfast in the faith. What may seem life's unmangeables may in reality be quite manageable if we would only do what God has told us to do.

I have yet to see old Clyde Beatty put his jungle cats through their paces, but I've seen some first-class devil tamers at work. These are dedicated Christians who have stood up to Satan and resisted. Thank God for the resisters!

Self-appointed Examiners

Who art thou that judgest another man's servant? to his own master he standeth or falleth. —Romans 14:4

While reading God's Word, I noted that somehow the Corinthian Christians had fallen into a rut of testing the sincerity of another's faith. The strange thing about the Corinthians was that the man whose faith was in question was none other than the apostle Paul. Writing to them, the apostle reminded them that it might be well for them to look to themselves as to whether they were really in Christ or not: "It is yourselves that you should be testing," he wrote, "not me."

One of the easiest things in the world to get bogged down in is suspecting another Christian of some sinister motive. Just because we may have had a bad experience with a Christian brother sometime in the past, we must not get stuck in foreboding suspicions in our relationships with other fellow Christians. Faith in God necessitates trust in His children.

It is easy to predict the results of living in constant suspicion of other Christians. One, it makes life generally miserable. Two, the suspicion usually is projected to others, resulting in an infection of the whole. Suspicion cannot be hidden. It is transmitted in several little unconscious ways: body language, verbal inflection, and subconscious innuendo. Feeling the suspicion, the brother in Christ becomes discouraged and often is defeated in his efforts to grow up in the family of God.

I knew someone once who was so suspicious of his fellow Christians he just couldn't trust anyone. Occasionally his mistrust would be justified, but what about all the rest? Subjecting them to his various "tests," he demeaned them and demoralized them. How much better for all the brethren, including himself, would it have been if he would have put himself to the test first. Maybe seeing the plank in his own eye, he wouldn't have been so up-tight over the sawdust in his brother's eye.

I don't know of many great Christians who have clawed and climbed their way up and over a church full of suspicious and doubting examiners. Most of the great Christians I know were cradled and nurtured in a church of believers who have loved with a love that is patient and kind.

So what if one time in a hundred someone does prove untrustworthy? It would seem to me that, from a statistical standpoint alone, it would be better to be wrong once in a hundred times, than wrong ninety-nine times out of a hundred.

Parable of the Stolen Rock

That ye, always having all sufficiency in all things, may abound to every good work. —2 Corinthians 9:8

To secure his property, a man converted all his assets into one huge diamond. The man then hid his precious stone in a secret place, which he would inspect regularly. This unusual activity aroused the curiosity of an observer. Suspecting there was a hidden treasure, the observer went to the no-longer-secret place and stole the diamond.

When the rightful owner returned and saw that the diamond was gone, he wept and tore his hair. A neighbor, hearing the reason of the man's extravagant grief, went to him and consoled him with these words: "Don't sweat it, man! All you have to do is put any old rock in the hiding place, and then think of it as your precious diamond. If you never meant to use your possession, the one will do you as much good as the other."

The moral of this updated fable is quite clear. The worth of a man's treasure is not in its possession, but in its use. The same can be said for talent and time. The value is not in how much we have, but how much we use what we have.

Jesus' teaching in the parable of the pounds crystallizes the same truth: what is not used is taken away.

Now, it occurs to me that with this truth we have a diamond of great worth. We can do with it one of two things. We can find a secret place in our minds to hide it away, or we can put it to use so that others might see our good works and glorify God. If we hide it away we risk losing it, but if we use it we enjoy it forever.

Christian stewardship is not possessing but

using properly what is possessed. All that we have—talents, time, and treasure—are gifts from God. The knowledge that failure to use such gifts results in loss is a precious gem given to us of God. Let us therefore use this asset, along with our other assets, to His glory and for our enjoyment.

What value is there in owning long years of time if they are to be squandered eyeballing a "boob-tube"? There is no value in holding tightly to great sums of money, for whose shall the money be when we are dead and gone? What gain is there in possession of talents unused and unspent? They, too, shall be stolen eventually by the archfoe, death. What good is it to know this truth and then hide it until it is forgotten? Truth, time, talent, and treasure are all assets to be used for God's glory, not just to be possessed. The miracle of God's divine economy is that they are never exhausted in using them to His glory. In hiding them, they are soon taken away.

Born on "Want Day"

When I became a man, I put away childish things.
—1 Corinthians 13:11

One day I heard a friend say, "I must have been born on 'Want Day.' "

The wailing of a child crying, "I wa-a-nt," is to be expected of little children. The shame of it is that parents have indulged the wants of their children, and the children have grown up to be pampered darlings still bawling, "I want! I want!"

It seems an awful lot of us have been born on "Want Day." No sooner than we satisfy one want, we have developed two to take its place. The one that was so important the day before is relegated to an accumulation of unused and unappreciated dust catchers, place fillers, or tax liabilities. Bored with things, the next step is to want flings. That is the point where homes become broken, faith is fractured, and hopes are shattered.

We are ruined, not by what we really want, but by what we think we want. We often find ourselves overspending for that which neither fills nor satisifes the longing of the human heart. Men have advanced all sorts of solutions to this "I want it" syndrome, but none seem quite as apropos as Paul's admonition, "Quit you like men, be strong." The answer is in growing up to the ability to harmonize our wants with God's will. When that happens, people will find that they spend less and less time wasting their labor for that "I wa-a-nt," which perishes with the obtaining.

The next time we feel that childish "I wa-a-nt" coming on, let us quit ourselves like adults, determining if it's worth the sacrifice of life, marriage, children, and maybe even our souls.

Monkey See, Monkey Do

He that keepeth his mouth keepeth his life.
—Proverbs 13:3

In a family "rap session" recently, we were discussing the "common talk" so widely used in our present culture. Our lament was how it was affecting all of us, young and old, causing many to fall into the same speech patterns of the world around us. It is frightening to contemplate how completely, in such a few short years, the crass, crude, vulgar, irreverent, and abusive language has become so faithfully aped by so many.

Verbal filth pours out of people's mouths like raw sewage pours into a metropolitan disposal plant. The vast difference is that most sewage treatment plants have the mission of abolishing something like eighty percent of the harmful effects of raw sewage; but there is no provision for nullifying the harmful qualities of verbal sewage dumped into the daily atmosphere of the average person. Without the love of parents who care, a church that dares to point to the danger of such pollution, and a community committed to excellence, people just accept obscenity and blasphemy as an accepted and even desirable way of communication. No wonder that sewer-talk is on the increase. Virtually every book is crammed full of it, and every movie tries to outdo the previous one in using the most shocking vulgarities! The excuse, of course, is realism, and they do have a point. Most of the novels and movies are about prostitutes, homosexuals, whoremongers, God-haters, the criminally oriented, sadists, psychopaths, and grossly angry or unhappy people, wildly indignant or frustrated about something or everything.

Now, the real puzzler is how so many good folk seem to want to ape these weird half-wits they read about and see portrayed in the movies they see, rated "GP," "X," "R," and "F" (flunked out). It seems that so many people in today's culture have for their heroes some strange characters. In mimicking the sounds they read and hear they are in effect saying to a waiting world, "Look, don't let my education, church affiliation, or high birth throw you off. I am just as common, crass, and profane as the next person."

Let us remember that we are born of God, reared in a family whose requirement is excellence, and educated to good manners and clean speech. Let us as Christians refuse the temptation to mimic the style and speech of the unrefined, uneducated, and unredeemed who have no standards of excellence or motivation to reach beyond a monkey see, monkey do level of behavior.

One antipollution move that our young and old alike can accomplish in our time is to turn off all the verbal sewage we keep dumping out of our mouths. The only people I know who are impressed by common talk are common livers. Who wants to be identified with the prostitutes, perverts, and psychopaths, except to raise them to a higher standard of life? Many folk who are not any of the above, do not have the good sense to refuse to be identified with the same.

We need to be reminded of Paul's words, "If ye then be risen with Christ, seek those things which are above, . . . Set your affection on things above, not on things on the earth" (Colossians 3:1, 2).

Paint and People

For we are his workmanship, created in Christ Jesus unto good works. —Ephesians 2:10

The greased pig has been caught, the last proud pony has been shown, and the last harness race has been run. Ribbons for all kinds of excellence have been distributed to competitors in everything from jam-making to cattle breeding. The county fair is over. Its tents have been struck, the gaily-lit rides dismantled, the gift stands are gone, and with them the smell of popcorn and coneys.

The whole thing that is now a touch of the past no one is willing to let pass for all time. As long as there are skills or crafts, and an interest in improving or excelling, let there be county fairs where progress can be noted and accomplishments recorded.

To me, a special interest in fairs has been in the fine arts division. Like most people, I have wondered at times about the judges in some of the selections they make. It seems to me that too many of the first choices in painting were based on those entries which bore the least possible resemblance to anything mineral or animal, living or dead, past, present, or future.

Artists have assured me that art is not necessarily an expression of something that looks like something else. Art is the creation of something that is unique and altogether different from anything else. Out of such "creativity" the beholder sees for himself what he wants to see.

Dabbling with paints and brush, I decided that, judging from some of the pictures I had seen ribbons on in past fairs, maybe I could do a little creating of my own. I thus busied myself in experimenting during some spare time. As a result, I came up with an exciting new art technique which I call an "acrylic wash." A picture can be produced in a matter of minutes instead of hours of hard, detailed work. It requires no discipline at all in learning, practicing, or improving. In fact, the less the artist does, the better the results. This is my secret, in three easy steps:

(1) Take a canvas art board and smear at least four different colors of acrylic paint over its surface.

(2) Let stand for one minute, then dump one cup of cold water on the painted surface.

(3) Let the water mix slightly with the paint, and then drain the water off—horizontally for a horizontal picture, vertically for a vertical one. Presto! An instant abstract and a winner! (Mine won an "Honorable Mention.")

One thing I learned in my new interest in abstracts is that undirected paint is like undirected lives. The loose paint may create some interesting color; but more often than not its final form comes out either grotesque, with demonic forms and shapes, or extremely muddy from the haphazard mixing of the colors.

Paint needs the creativity of a skilled and knowledgeable artist to give it beauty or form. The same is true of life. That is why we so desperately need God to give us direction. In our own doing what we want, we wind up grossly muddy or grotesquely shaped.

You are the paint, the Bible is the brush, and God is the artist. But there is a weakness in this analogy. In this case the Artist doesn't direct the paint without the consent of the paint!

Habakkuk's Spigot

Serve the Lord with gladness.   *—Psalm 100:2*

Some people have questioned any display of emotion in Christian worship. The verbal "Amen," shouts of praise, or hands clapped in support of what has been said or done, often is met with the icy stares of those unaccustomed to such out-breaks within the church.

It isn't any wonder that many churches discourage outward expressions of agreement, joy, or other strong feeling during the services. For years Christian brethren have been conditioned to suppress the emotions. A single Old Testament passage, "The Lord is in his holy temple: let all the earth keep silence before him" (Habakkuk 2:20), has been repeated and reprinted thousands of times. I suppose this was to induce a reverence for God and His house. In doing this, however, the pendulum has swung so far to the side of awe and respect that human emotion in worship has been shut off, like a spigot.

This is most unfortunate, because the meaning of the word "emotion" means to "move out," "stir up," or "agitate." There is, of course, a time for keeping silence before the Lord; but there is also a time for emoting, for feeling, for moving. Man is an emotional being. He feels sorrow, joy, and anger. Man's relationship to his Creator should help him to express these emotions and properly channel them, not suppress them. Let us show, in positive ways, a love of God. This moves others to love! Let us express righteous anger over sin. This stirs people to direct anger rightly and properly. Let us demonstrate the joy of life in Christ. This may agitate men into joyous living. God gave us emotions to "move," "stir up," and "agitate." Worship should do just that!

Although we are always being warned that the taste for emotional displays may become a dangerous taste, I am convinced that by shutting off our emotions completely we can easily become humorless, rigid, and stereotyped. We shall then be more like programmed robots than human beings with feelings.

Some Scriptures that we ought to give as much attention to as that solemn and lone passage in Habakkuk are:

"Be glad in the Lord, and *rejoice,* ye righteous: and *shout* for joy, all ye that are upright in heart" (Psalm 32:11).

"Sing unto him a new song; play skilfully with a *loud* noise" (Psalm 33:3).

"O *clap your hands,* all ye people; *shout* unto God with the voice of triumph" (Psalm 47:1).

"Thus will I bless thee while I live: I will *lift up my hands* in thy name" (Psalm 63:4).

"O bless our God, ye people, and *make the voice of his praise to be heard"* (Psalm 66:8).

Such Scripture passages are just a few of the many that show worship as something emotional, i.e., with feeling, capable of moving men, stirring them up, agitating them to a celebration of life and joy in the Giver of life.

That "silence" passage in Habakkuk was not meant for turning off the spigot of emotional expression in worship, but rather for shutting the mouths that are running off about everything else under the sun but God.

God's Family No Different

Bear ye one another's burdens, and so fulfil the law of Christ. —Galatians 6:2

When I visited recently with a very alert and spiritually sensitive young couple, some insights surfaced in which all of us need to share. The young husband had been disillusioned with much of the behavior he had observed coming from professing Christians. He couldn't understand how a religious faith that had been around for so many centuries had been unable to make more of an impact upon its followers. He had seen so much bigotry, insensitivity, and lovelessness out of the "born again" that he had about concluded he would rather not be associated with such a family.

All of us can sympathize with this feeling because all have been embarrassed at times by the behavior of fellow Christians. We have wondered how come some Christians can be so immature, how the "faith once and for all delivered to the saints," after being around for so many centuries, can be so ineffective in bringing about a change for the good.

Some truths that we discovered are as follows:

First, the faith "once and for all delivered" is not accumulative. We do not have any two-thousand-year-old Christians sharing their wisdom of such maturity and experience. Christians, like all men, die physically. The "faith," therefore, must depend upon the newborn Christians to take the place of mature Christians who pass from the scene. Because of this constantly changing membership, the church has to keep on learning the same old lessons, over and over, every generation.

We often criticize God's family for what we tolerate in every other family, i.e., family members being in different stages of development. The household of God also can point to members in all stages of development. Some are infants, without strength or experience. Others, like toddlers, are into everything, some of which they shouldn't be. Others are like those active Primaries or Juniors, whose energy outstrips their judgment, or like preteens, who act like their hands are all thumbs and their feet weigh a hundred pounds each. Some Christians are like adolescents, terribly self-conscious, fiercely independent, but dependent for so much. There are those who are mature, some more than others. There are some who are retarded, and some others who cannot seem to function within the framework of the family or society at all.

Somehow we accept the differences in members of a family without condemning the family. It should be the same within the church. Yet, here we expect perfection, although there are no perfect Christians, and never will be this side of Heaven. All are sinners saved by grace.

Because of the ever-changing situation and because we do not inherit goodness, the church will always be made up of sinners saved by grace. But, imperfect as our Christian family may be, the world is a better place because of it.

We must never chuck the church because its ever-changing, ever-learning members behave in the way their particular stage of development or underdevelopment dictates. We just have to accept each other in the same way God does, with the strong supporting the weak, and all bearing one another's burdens.

I have a hunch that when we all get involved in understanding and helping one another, our faults, failures, and immaturities will not loom so large as to deny the family which Christ purchased with His own blood.

The Condemning Clerk

Judge not, that ye be not judged.   *—Matthew 7:1*

At our morning coffee break, an office visitor told us of her retirement as an employee at the State School, after thirty years of service. Someone asked just what her work was. She replied that she was a "condemning clerk." That title raised everybody's interest and curiosity.

"A condemning clerk?" I asked. "What on earth does a condemning clerk do?"

"Well," our visitor answered, "A condemning clerk goes around condemning things."

After twenty-three years in church work, I have observed a lot of condemning and listened to a lot of condemning. I didn't know until now that there was an official title for it. Think of it: an official condemning clerk sitting right here in the church office describing her work as "going around condemning things." Amazing are the ways of men!

For many years the state of Illinois had found it helpful to have on its payroll a condemning clerk. Her job, of course, was to condemn obsolete and worn-out supplies and equipment so that the replacements could be issued and secured. Chalk one up for Caesar. The state is more wise than the children of light. Their "condemning clerks" have official status, and they are *expected* to "go around condemning things."

Now, the church has its condemning clerks, too, but their work never has been recognized. It is true that there is little difference in the two. While one may be condemning worn brooms, cracked dishes, or frayed bed linens, the other condemns the minister, most of the programs, and all of the decisions of the church board. They condemn the music, the young people, and all those other people who do not smell, dress, or look as they should. They condemn the sinking or the rising of the budget, whichever the case may be. They condemn the sermons for being too "pricky," teaching for being too "thicky," and the fellowship for being too "cliquey." They condemn by anonymous notes and by calls one to another. They condemn at work, at play, or wherever there may be an ear, or two, or more.

Summer or winter, rain, snow, or sleet, the condemners come through. There is no telling what good comes of the spirits that are crushed, the programs that are squelched, the would-be Christians that are turned off and away by the "high calling" that some aspire to.

I propose that we learn from Caesar. Let us render unto him the things that are his, and from this day on elect an official condemning clerk to do all the condemning. If the program is no good, let the condemning clerk scrap the old leader and bring in a new one. If members don't cut their hair right, vote right, or come from the right families, let the condemning clerk excommunicate them and requisition some new ones more in keeping with our tender taste for what's proper and chic.

What the church needs to help equip the saints is an *official* "condemning clerk," who would take his place among the apostles, prophets, evangelists, ministers, and teachers. Think of it! Everything and everyone in church who is not right, the condemning clerk can officially condemn and throw out!

Perhaps you know of someone you would like to recommend for the job. Better still, next time you hear someone condemning, you might suggest that he or she might apply for the job.

It is plain to see that an official "condemning clerk" is what every church needs. I wonder why someone has never thought of it before. Come to think of it, maybe they have! John's Gospel tells of a woman who was brought to Jesus and accused of adultery. Her accusers were ready to condemn her to death until Jesus brought up the little detail of letting him that is without sin cast the first stone. It is strange how the condemning clerks faded away, leaving our Lord asking the accused, "Where are they? Did no man condemn thee?" Hearing the woman's answer that there were none, the Lord said, "Neither do I condemn thee: go thy way; from henceforth sin no more."

Well, I still think it would be a good idea to have an official condemning clerk, if we could just find *someone who's qualified!*

Looking Outward

Lift up your eyes, and look on the fields; for they are white already to harvest.   —John 4:35

It is strange how something that is said can lodge in one's memory, even though the author may have been forgotten. Someone spoke to a new church group of which I was a part, and warned us of the three stages of church growth. In stage one, he said, the members of a new church joyously *talk to others* about the good news of Christ. In stage two, the brethren will spend most of their time *talking to each other* about methods and needs. In stage three they regress into *talking about each other,* each blaming the other for all that fizzles, flops, or fades.

There is, of course, more truth to this little three-point homily than anyone wants to admit. The result is a regression that moves from a talking to others about God to a talking about others who are created in the image of God! Such is a crisis that borders on spiritual bankruptcy.

It is so easy to move from one stage to another. The idealism of sharing one's faith seems too often to succumb to the temptation of just sharing one's expertise with those of a like precious faith. That is all right, except that from that stage it is but one step down to a carping criticism of what seems to be the brethren's lack of either faith or expertise.

Stage three, talking about others, has a paralyzing effect on the whole body of Christ. Each member is fearful of acting or introducing something new, for fear of being shot down. Everyone has real doubts about bringing their friends to a church in which they have heard so much criticism by those who are the membership.

Ego trips, induced by talking about others, are heady drugs often maintained by people who wouldn't dream of indulging in booze or barbiturates. The results, nevertheless, are similar; both destroy the effectiveness of the user, and at the same time unleash the forces of alienation, which rip and tear at the fiber of the community.

What stage the church may be entering might not be too difficult to determine, seeing that we spend many hours talking to each other, and so few hours talking to others. Lest we be tempted to slip into the catastrophic "stage three" of talking about each other, I would suggest that each of us adopt this resolution: every time we are tempted to criticize a brother or sister for *anything,* we will instead direct that energy to finding someone with whom to share our faith. It may be that in talking with others about the good news of Christ, we will not need to discuss the bad news of frailties and imperfections.

What Is Love?

By this shall all men know that ye are my disciples, if ye have love one to another. —John 13:35

A schoolteacher brought into my office a stack of third-grade essays on the subject, "What Is Love?" One can almost see those wheels turning and gears meshing together as those budding intellectuals pondered their assignment and reviewed their experiences to come up with appropriate answers.

One boy defined love as "liking someone a lot," but later had second thoughts and added, "Love isn't just liking. It is an extroirdranary (extraordinary) hunger out of your heart." That out of the mouths of babes should come such wisdom is a sight worth turning aside to see. Many adults who do not have children or grandchildren might have difficulty understanding the depth of this definition of love. That boy put his finger on something real. Love *is* a hunger out of one's heart. It is a hunger to be with, to enjoy, and to cherish. Love is a heart hunger.

Another third-grader defined love as being "very sweat." I rather imagine that in this instance little Karen meant "sweet," but surely "sweat" is better! Why? Because most love worth the use of the term produces sweat. Love is hard work. It is caring, sacrificing, and giving. It is expensive. Hard effort is expended that the object of our love might be beautified and honored, in keeping with our devotion.

The Bible tells us about God's love for us: "For God so loved the world, that he gave his only begotten Son." Man! There is the effort and the price of love. I don't know why God could love us so much. "And being in an agony he [Jesus] prayed more earnestly: and his sweat was as it were great drops of blood falling down to the ground'' (Luke 22:44). Love is hard, and it is costly.

Seeing how much He has loved us, how much have we loved Him? Have we yet cared enough, or given enough, or sacrificed enough to raise a sweat? Have we felt for Christ the same heart hunger that we have for our children or children's children? These are legitimate questions that need to be asked because love, to be real love, is a reciprocal thing. It is shared, felt, and shown by both sides. Brethren, because He has first loved us, let us love Him. Love is a heart hunger! Love is sweat! It is God's and yours!

Letting In the Pets?

Be not deceived: evil companionships corrupt good morals. —1 Corinthians 15:33; ASV

Thirteen-month-old Carla Graves was asleep on the sofa. Her mother smiled at the sleeping child, then she went to the back door to let in the family's two pet puppies. Opening the door, Mrs. Graves was literally knocked aside by a big Doberman Pinscher that bounded into the house on the heels of the puppies. Making straight for the sofa, the strange dog viciously attacked little Carla, dragging her from the sofa, inflicting serious lacerations on her face and forehead. Mrs. Graves snatched the child from the dog, fighting off the dog's attacks upon her, and was finally able to retreat from the house, locking the dog inside.

Mrs. Graves called the police from a neighbor's house. When they came, they overtranquillized the big dog and it died. The child will live, but she will need extensive plastic surgery as a result of the fierce attack.

The story is one filled with horror, both for Carla and her mother. One can hardly imagine a more terrifying experience than having one's home invaded by a strange and fierce beast that would rush in and attack a sleeping child. Who would have thought such sheer terror could have come bounding in with the family pets?

There is a parallel here. I couldn't help wondering what hurt we may subject our children to when we open the door to our pet sins. So many things we allow or indulge in seem so harmless, like playful puppies. The harm is not with the pet puppies or the pet sins, but rather in the company they keep. In many cases, parents (or governments) thought they were opening the door to only some playful pets. But who knows what injury was loosed upon the unsuspecting children of the world, to be ripped and torn by the unleashed fury of that which bounded in with the pets? It's not so much the pet sins; it's the company they keep.

The strength of a parable is for one to draw his or her own conclusions.

(Story based on news article by Thomas Keating, staff writer for *Indianapolis Star*.)

Practicing What We Preach

My little children, let us not love in word, neither in tongue; but in deed and in truth.   *–1 John 3:18*

Because of the successes of science's antibiotics, many people mistakenly believe all ills can be cured in short order. When stubborn diseases resist medicine's modern miracles, the healers and the sick alike are impatient for some potent pill or potion.

Church leaders and churchmen alike suffer the same kind of impatience in dealing with spiritual ills. Many, in their impatience, begin to think that all this old dying world needs for its recovery is the "gos-pill," which to them is some kind of super-pill for all that's wrong with the world. Go, tell the world, "Jesus saves," and flap! Wham! Pop! The sin-sick people are suddenly healed and a dying world is saved. It is not that way, is it? The feverish and unsound world glances our way and comments, "Jesus we've heard of, but who are *you?*"

There is no doubt as to the power of the gospel to save. It is a pungent potion. Distributing the gospel is an important, vital mission of the church. Yet, *living* the gospel is equally important. Few people are going to take the medicine one is prescribing, if the proclaimer is as stricken as those he is trying to save.

There is more to the gospel than declaring it. Only when the dying see its power to give healing to loveless, depressed, short-tempered, cruel, unbelieving, arrogant, and intemperate people, will they take seriously any claims that it is a healing for the nations. The mission of the church is to evangelize, yes, but we must also live up to the gospel that we preach.

The Gospel According to You

Ye are our epistle written in our hearts, known and read of all men.
                                        –2 Corinthians 3:2

Has it ever occurred to you that you are the best Christian someone else knows? In fact, you may be the *only* Christian someone knows. Whether you are young or old, male or female, black or white, rich or poor, you may indeed be the best, or the only Christian someone else knows.

The apostle Paul once told the Corinthian Christians that they were an epistle (letter) "written not with ink, but with the Spirit of the living God." Paul said that such letters were known and read of all men.

As believers in Christ, we become the letters of the Holy Spirit, and someone else is reading us. In other words, there may be some child, or youth, or fellow-worker who lives in close relation to you, who never, never reads an epistle of Paul, James, John, or other men inspired of the Holy Spirit to pen the New Covenant. These same people, whoever they are, may never, never have been introduced to a single great saint of either the Old or New Testament. Their only visible illustration or demonstration of God's message is that which you show. To them you are the epistle "known and read of all men."

I must frankly confess that the knowledge of this truth is rather nerve-shattering. Here I am, imperfect as I am, nevertheless a living letter written of the Holy Spirit, known and read by all those who come in contact with me. I may be the best and only Christian someone knows. What an awesome responsibility!

Or is it my responsibility? If the letter is of the

Holy Spirit, why isn't it His responsibility? The truth is, it *is* His responsibility to help me be the person that, when read by others, will glorify God. But there is a hitch. I must be open to the Spirit's guiding hand. My heart must be exposed to the writing hand.

If that someone sees me as the only or the best Christian he knows, the question is, what kind of message has he from God? Have I muddled his thinking, confused his reasoning, or discouraged his further inquiry into the things of God? Each of us must consider these things in relation to our influence. If we have confused the message for our readers, it must be that we have shoved too much of ourselves into the epistle.

God is not the author of confusion. If someone is getting a confused picture of what God is like from reading our epistle, it must be because we haven't been willing to give the Spirit a clean sheet to write on. The smudges and pollution have to be erased away by the blood of Christ. The heart has to be opened to the hand of God. It is then that the Spirit can write a great epistle, not on tablets of stone, "but in fleshy tablets of the heart." When those "somebodies" read the Holy Spirit messages that are written on your heart, then they are led to look deeper into other epistles like Corinthians, Ephesians, Philippians, etc., and in them are the words of life!

Are you important? Whenever you doubt it, remember this: You are the best Christian someone knows. Say, what is the message of the Holy Spirit according to you? It is God's responsibility to write the message. It is our responsibility to provide the life for Him to write.

A Touch of Heartburn

Keep thy heart with all diligence; for out of it are the issues of life. —*Proverbs 4:23*

It is sad to see how many imaginative children, with a capacity for high creativity, degenerate into tediously dull adults.

It is sad, too, to see bright-spirited youth planning to be married, aglow with dreams of love's fulfillment, later on dragging through married life in a state of hateful alienation.

Another sad thing is the devolution of other promising human relationships, such as waning neighborliness, diminishing friendships, or subsiding brotherhood.

What causes Christians to falter in love? Friends to drift apart? Neighbors to quit being neighborly? Husbands and wives to break up? Little children to lose interest in creativity?

Somehow, I think the answers are all related. Children lose interest in creating when there is little or no interest shown in what they have created. Husbands and wives break up when one or the other is all preoccupied with his or her own special interest. Neighbors lose interest in each other when neighboring makes demands or fails to meet demands. Friendships ebb pretty much for the same reason. The cost of caring reaches the point of being too great to bear comfortably. As for an abating brotherhood, add up the reasons for failing friendships, decreasing neighborliness, faltering marriages, and diminishing creativity in children, and you have an explanation for estrangement among Christians: people's self-centeredness.

Everyone wants to be encouraged, happily married, a part of a friendly neighborhood, have a host of close friends, and live within a close-knit spiritual family. The potential is there, for the world is full of willing people. Some people are willing to work for such an ideal, and the rest are willing to let them.

Of course, herein is the rub. Any human relationship requires caring, the kind of caring that motivates effort. The relationship that falters and fails is always the result of some working at it and some not. The world is full of willing people, some willing to work, and the rest willing to let them.

Shall those who are willing to work quit because others don't care or don't want to pay the price? I guess that all depends on whether one believes that a child's creativity is worth encouraging, a marriage is worth saving, a neighborhood is worth salvaging, a friendship is worth keeping, or a brother is worth the cost of caring. If there is no worth in such things, then why work? If there is great worth in them, why should it always be the other fellow's responsibility?

Food for thought? Yes, and it is a bit upsetting. One cannot help having a touch of heartburn while reflecting on what may have been, had we been more willing to work and less willing to let others carry the burden alone. You know, we need not have heartburn or failing relations. There is an antidote. It is effort, or work: "Work, for the night is coming."

Dumped With the Garbage

He sent his word, and healed them, and delivered them from their destructions. —Psalm 107:20

I read of a young couple in Indianapolis who experienced a horrid weekend. Married for two years, they had saved to make a belated honeymoon trip to Hawaii. On Friday the husband drew $1,400 out of the bank, for they had planned that the first thing on Monday he would buy the air tickets and put the rest into traveler's checks.

Worried about having that much cash in the apartment over the weekend, the young husband wrapped the fourteen one-hundred-dollar bills in some aluminum foil and put them in the refrigerator. He thought this would surely be the last place burglars would look for a cash hoard. Besides, he thought, if the house should catch on fire, the cash would be saved.

The young man went to work on Saturday morning, confident that all was safe, although he had failed to mention to his wife what he had done. She, not having to work on Saturday, decided it would be a good time to throw out the leftovers in the refrigerator. Finding the aluminum-wrapped package and noticing the green inside, she assumed it was some spoiled cheese and quickly threw it in the garbage.

The husband returned from work at noon and immediately checked the refrigerator for his hidden hoard, only to discover it gone! Explaining what she had thought the package was, they both raced to the back of the apartment to retrieve the money. The garbage cans were all empty! In a state near shock, the couple tried to find the superintendent of the building. He was away. The custodian was sick. No one knew the name of the scavenger company that had hauled off the apartment's trash. Someone thought the name of the company started with a D.

The couple phoned all the scavenger companies, and hit pay dirt with a "D. and J. Scavenger Company." However, the owner was the only one who knew the whereabouts of the truck that had picked up the trash. After many calls the owner finally was located, and he informed the couple that the truck in question was on its way to a landfill in Zionsville at that very moment.

The husband jumped into his car and made a mad rush to the dump. Arriving there, he waited for the truck. He waited some more. Time dragged on. At last he found a pay phone, and learned that the truck had sprung an oil leak. It was now in a service station. Rushing to the station, the now ragged newlywed learned that it would be Monday before the truck could be repaired and dumped. Hopes dimmed. It was a long, long weekend.

Monday finally came, and with it the couple watched the repaired truck pull into the dump and dislodge its load. Tons of heaped-up, pressed-together trash and garbage tumbled onto the soggy, rain-drenched landfill. There, in the stench and mess of it all, was the load that the couple were to pick through in the hope of finding one foil-wrapped package, no larger than a package of moldy cheese, but containing fourteen one-hundred-dollar bills. As they were about to begin, the husband looked at his feet and his eye caught a glimpse of a familar object. It was the used foil he had used to wrap the money. Sticking out of one end were the fourteen bills—wet, smelly, and dirty—but found!

Now, what does all this have to do with Christians? Only this, it is a modern parable. To that young couple, that money was agonizingly important. It represented the investment of long hours of work. It was the means of realizing a two-year dream. Both hours and dreams would have been wasted had the money not been found. The money never would have been found, had it not been for their dogged determination to find that which was lost.

What do you suppose would happen in a community where the people of God were as determined in searching for lost souls—lost souls which had been picked up, pressed together, hauled off, and dumped at the edge of Hell? My guess would be that the church might have some soggy, smelly, and not-too-pretty members, but there would be rejoicing in Heaven.

Another thing we might learn in this true story: Don't put either savings or Christians in cold storage where they could be mistakenly identified and thrown out as moldy cheese.

(Story based on news article by Thomas Keating, staff writer for *Indianapolis Star*.)

The Unwelcome Guest

Honour all men. —1 Peter 2:17

Thunder throws our dog, Charlie Brown, into a dog sweat (heavy panting). She (Her masculine name was given her by her not-too-observant previous owners) seeks human company at the first drop of the barometer. If entry to our house is not immediately available, she runs in a state of panic through the neighborhood, seeking any door that might be opened to her. The only requirement is that there be some person on the other side of that door. It doesn't matter who is there, just so there is someone. That person can be friendly or hostile. For her, any shelter is a shelter in the time of storm. Scold her, beat her, nothing less than bodily removal can force her to face the scepter of nature's threat, once she is inside what she deems her ark of safety.

Poor Charlie Brown! She doesn't realize that she is probably in far greater danger at the hands of those people with whom she seeks refuge and comfort, than she would be out in the storm. People concerned about expensive furniture and costly decor more often than not are unsympathetic toward wet, frightened, short-legged, long-haired dogs. Really, that's not too hard to understand. A strange, smelly, muddy, yellow mut (yellow inside and out) could be an expensive guest. We can accept the fact that people may be upset with such a situation and use whatever force is necessary to evict such an unwanted animal. The thing that is hard to understand, though, is the rejection some church members exert upon other human beings who, sweating out personal storms, have run to the church as an ark of safety.

Now, church folk seldom pick up a broom to chase out the undesirables. That is a method to be used on dirty and smelly dogs. We deal with people differently. We use more subtle means to get rid of frightened and undesirable people seeking the comfort of Christian fellowship. We devise nuances that cleverly and inaudibly, yet effectively, express our finding certain people unacceptable. We engineer stage whispers, which are meant to be overheard by the undesirables. We scorn, belittle, or make fun of any effort that they might attempt. We laugh in our accepted circles about how funny they appear or how "dumb" their comments are.

Frightened people are different from frightened dogs. Some things are worse for them than the storms. One thing more fearful is the rejection of those in whom they had hoped to find strength. For them it is better to face the night with all of its thunder, wind, and chill than to face the coldheartedness of the strong who have no fears.

The Liberating Force

Ye shall know the truth, and the truth shall make you free.
–John 8:32

Writing in large script so that King George would be sure to read his signature, John Hancock signed the *Declaration of Independence,* on July 4, 1776. Largely the work of Thomas Jefferson, the *Declaration of Independence* has been hailed the world over as a declaration of human freedom.

Long before this historical document came into being, God was laboring in Heaven and on earth to make men free. God created man free to move from place to place, and He made man free to choose between good and evil. Into the hands of this man, free to move and choose, God placed the original declaration of human freedom: the Bible! Jesus said, "Ye shall know the truth, and the truth shall make you free."

For fifty years the Communist government has been attacking and suppressing this truth of God. Churches have been closed; teachers of the Word have been persecuted; books on and about the truth of God have been banned or burned. Yet, in spite of the banning and the burning, the liberating power of God's truth still crops up in the USSR.

Consider the case of Alexander Solzhenitsyn, who without doubt is the most famous contemporary Russian novelist. A Nobel Prize winner, Solzhenitsyn now has written a book entitled, *August 1914.* He explains why his book could not be published in Russia: "Because of censorship for reasons inconceivable to the normal human mind, and were it for no other reason; because it would be necessary to write the word God in lower case; but I cannot lower myself to that—" In the book the author describes God as "the highest meaningful force in the universe."

How can one who has lived all his life under atheistic Communism have come to such a conclusion? Simple. Somehow, some way, through a crack in that iron curtain, the liberating force of truth has broken asunder the chains that once held this man in personal, civil, and political slavery. The editor of the *Indianapolis Star,* commenting on Mr. Solzhenitsyn's freedom within a slave state wrote, "God moves in a mysterious way, His wonders to perform."

I don't know about you, but right now I am very thankful for the *Declaration of Independence* and the document that inspired it: the original declaration of human freedom, called God's Holy Bible!

Marshmallow Mentality

God hath not given us the spirit of fear; but of power, and of love, and of a sound mind. —2 Timothy 1:7

Some time ago, the General Mills Company announced a program by which it agreed to redeem the coupons on its cereal boxes for much-needed lung, heart, and kidney machines. As most people know, these lifesaving machines are terribly expensive and are in short supply.

The company did manage to purchase and give away two hundred of the machines before some soft-headed protesters denounced General Mills for "trading in misery." Bowing to this public pressure, the company stopped redeeming its coupons for the desperately needed machines and returned to its long-standing practice of giving away forks and spoons.

How wondrous are the ways of mankind! It is some kind of lunacy that would reason that redeeming coupons for forks and spoons is better than exchanging them for life-giving heart, lung, and kidney machines. It is a marshmallow mentality that would make one bow to this kind of soft-headed public pressure and abandon a truly humanitarian project.

Poor General Mills! The company is caught in the middle, criticized because it was doing something, then criticized because it stopped doing it. Somehow the whole thing illustrates the necessity for companies, government officials, and Christians to make decisions on what is morally right, rather than on what is expedient.

When decisions are made on the basis of what may be immediately advantageous, without regard for principles and values, that company, that government, or that individual is in trouble. Conviction of being right, based on positive and proven values, is the source of the starch that makes men resist the marshmallow heads whose thinking is more fluffy than solid.

Many of the tried-and-proven values and morals of yesterday are being scrapped today because too many people decide what is of value through the process of determining what is expedient. It is easy, therefore, to throw off what was once moral and valuable if it is no longer advantageous. God's right is still right. A decision made on that rightness is not so easily abandoned. Would to God more decisions among corporations, states, and just common folk like you and me, were based on what is right rather than on what may be expedient!

I'm all for the church's redeeming some jelly coupons for some starch. If there were enough such redemption, it would take more than a marshmallow mentality to bowl us over.

Return of the Apes

And this I pray, . . . that ye may approve things that are excellent. —Philippians 1:9, 10

It was bound to happen. In a recent art contest, a painting by a five-year-old won first place. Just imagine how demoralizing it would be to all the other artists to be beaten out of a contest by a five-year-old! Adding insult to injury was the fact that the five-year-old was an orangutan! The exhibit was entered into the contest under the name of D. James Orang. Zoo keepers were delighted with their charge's first-place award, but were apprehensive over his future. It seems that the famous artist eats all his paintbrushes!

There has to be something radically wrong with the cultural values of men, to have produced a battery of art critics who cannot distinguish between what is of ape and what is of man. It is frightening. With orangutans winning art contests, who knows what may be next? With D. James Orang becoming a famous artist, what is going to keep other orangutans from writing hit songs or best-selling novels? Judging from some of the latest hits I have heard and the novels I have read lately, it may have happened already. What a ghastly thought!

God expects more from man than what an orangutan can do, considerably more. We should re-evaluate, and start expecting men to produce works of excellency once again, works that can be identified positively as the results of talent, culture, and training. One of the prayers of the apostle Paul for the Philippians was that they might "approve the things that are excellent." That is what we ought to do, and when we do, once again excellency will prevail.

Who's Programming You?

Walk in the Spirit, and ye shall not fulfil the lust of the flesh. —Galatians 5:16

The human body is a remarkable creation. It is maintained by some ingenious systems that can be described only as marvelous and incredible in every design and detail.

Consider first the exceptional conversion system called the digestive system, converting raw material into energy that can be used immediately or stored for future use.

Ponder next the fantastic air-filtering system called the lungs, which sift out the usable properties from the unusable ones. Then the efficient conveyor system transports the usable materials throughout the body and carries the unusable ones to the various outlets.

Wonder of wonders is the body's pump, which works tirelessly twenty-four hours per day, day in and day out, sending life-giving blood to faraway tissues through miles and miles of arteries and veins.

On top of all these wonders is the body's communication system, which conveys complex messages with incredible speed to every member of the body. It functions automatically or manually, as the situation demands.

Greater than the nerves, heart, kidneys, lungs, or digestive system is the most awesome organ of all: the brain. Computer systems have been compared to a brain, but certainly man's brain is far ahead of anything it may invent or develop. Man's brain is God's creation. The brain not only stores quantities of information; it is capable of independently using its stored-up information creatively. Thus man is able to perform such unbelievable feats as sending men to the moon and back. It is this created computer that I want to discuss, this incredible, marvelous, and unique organ that is capable of so much.

Similar to the invented computer, the brain has to be programmed. How it is programmed will determine its usefulness, and whether it will be a bane or a blessing.

From infancy on, man's computer is being programmed. We are influenced for good or evil by whom we know or do not know; what we value or do not value; by whom we love or do not love.

The human mind that is programmed to know the Lord, value His Word, and love those created in His image, is programmed by the Holy Spirit. The results of this kind of programming are love, joy, peace, patience, kindness, generosity, fidelity, tolerance, and self-control.

On the other hand, the human mind may not know the Lord or value His Word. The thoughts of the owner may not extend to others. Such a mind is programmed by a different spirit, the spirit of self. Self dominates the desire, and it is the desire of the lower nature. The activities of the lower nature are obvious: sexual immorality, impurity of mind, sensuality, worship of false gods, witchcraft, hatred, quarreling, jealousy, bad temper, rivalry, factions, party spirit, envy, drunkenness, orgies, and things like that. The big question is, how much programming are we getting from the Holy Spirit and how much from the spirit of our lower nature? That depends on several factors: (1) what we know; (2) what we value; (3) whom we love.

Somehow, when you really think about this, Bible reading, Sunday school, and worship take on new importance. It is through these we are introduced to the Power that programs men for good: the Spirit of truth, the Holy Spirit.

Power for the People

They that wait upon the Lord shall renew their strength.
–Isaiah 40:31

What is it about power that so fascinates men? This insatiable desire drives men to insane lengths to lord it over others. Tyrants and would-be tyrants slaughter and devour to gain or retain power. How logical and right power-thirsting men make their ambitions appear! Drunk on their own importance, they offer the world their leadership as an elixir for all ills. Strange, isn't it, that none of the ills are ever cured by such cure-alls? Instead, we are plunged into bloodbaths of hate in which race is pitted against race, nation against nation, countryman against countryman, neighbor against neighbor, and even brother against brother.

Lovers of power offer us life, and give us death; prosperity, and give us poverty; freedom, and give us slavery. It has been that way in the past, and it always will be: Life, prosperity, and freedom are not the results of man's grabbing, conniving, blasting, pushing, and strutting for power. Life, prosperity, and freedom are the results of people of goodwill working cooperatively for the good of all.

When Jesus was born, the angelic host praised God, saying, "Glory to God in the highest, and on earth peace, good will toward men." Heralding the arrival of Israel's long-expected Messiah, the angels voiced the hope of men, then and now, that there be peace and goodwill toward men. What happened? Have the tyrants who keep killing the innocents won? Must the world spin out its destiny, ever listening to Rachel weep for her children? Is there yet hope in Him that came, born in a stable, the Prince of Peace?

I believe, of course, that there is hope, but hope is not wishful thinking. It is hard and difficult following peace's Prince into the path of peace. It has to start somewhere! Why not with you and with me? It calls for the abandoning of our little power plans. It means emptying ourselves as Christ empties himself. It means becoming obedient to the full counsel of God, even to the death of our cherished ideas of our own importance and rights. These may be our well-nursed resentments and grudges, our indulged envies and jealousies, our treasured ambitions, and even our dearly fostered avarice and covetousness.

I'm for "power for the people" all right, as long as it is God's power working through us. That is the power, and the only power I know that liberates, helps men to truly prosper, and leads us to the larger life to live!

> Come, Thou long-expected Jesus,
>   Born to set Thy people free;
> From our fears and sins release us;
>   Let us find our rest in Thee!
>
> By Thine own eternal Spirit
>   Rule in all our hearts alone;
> By Thine all-sufficient merit,
>   Raise us to Thy glorious throne.
>   *—Charles Wesley*

Peace! Shalom! *Pax vobiscum!*

What Is a Chirch?

Ye also are builded together for an habitation of God through the Spirit. —Ephesians 2:22

A friend who teaches third grade in Springfield, Illinois, knows how much I enjoy the comments of her pupils in the definitive essays she has them write. In her latest batch, there were some tremendous answers to the question, "What is a church?"

You can picture that class of forty-six pupils with lined paper before them and pencil in hand pondering how they would define a church. From the names on the papers, there is no doubt all faiths were represented there. All the pupils were uncritical, if not highly complimentary, of the church.

The spelling was not too precise in some cases, but there was understanding of what the church is all about! One little girl wrote: "Well, a chirch is where you learn about God and the bibull." It is too bad that both God and the Bible have been ruled out of the schools and ignored in most homes, but this little girl is right. The church does exist to teach us about God and the Bible.

In her paper, Staci sees the church as a place where "you wereship God and praise him" She sees churches as being "very pretty because they have peaple." Staci also observed that "some peaple go to a temple rather than a church, but no matter, God loves them."

Little John wrote that a church is a place to "pray and have fun." Somehow I was drawn to this paper like a steel filing to a magnet. John also said his church "is a place of love." If I lived in Springfield, I'd surely want to investigate John's church. Something there is A-OK, to have impressed that boy favorably with the conviction that a church is a place of love and a lot of fun.

Some of the youngsters really waxed theological. Bill put his finger on something important when he indicated that "church is a place where people pray with God and if you are hurt God will heal your hurt up." Beautiful, Bill! God does heal our hurts.

Suzanne didn't like the way "bad people yelled at Jesus and hung Him on a cross," but she said, "Christ rose again in glory" and, "God died on the cross for us."

Andrea wrote, "Church is a place where you sing and pray to Jesus and God . . . a place where you are happy."

In his description, Jeff says the church is a place to see God and Him to see you. If little Jeff is right on that score, God surely hasn't seen much of some folk I've known.

Chip saw the church as God's home, where "you learn about the creation of the world and Mozis."

One young writer touched this older writer's curiosity button to wonder what anxiety she may have developed over not being taken to church. She wrote, "A church is where people go to learn about God. Some people do not go to church and they do not learn about God." She seemed to express hope by adding, "That does not mean that God does not love you."

Jerilyn's comments certainly encouraged this old preacher's heart. She says that church is where "A pricher stands and talks to people and God listens to what the pricher says." There is no mention of the people listening, but at least God listens. That is some consolation!

Society's Glue

As ye would that men should do to you, do ye also to them likewise. —Luke 6:31

"Promises, promises, promises! All I hear is promises," roared the sales manager. Slamming his fist hard on the table to emphasize his next statement, he bellowed out, "What this organization needs is more results, not more promises!" He collected his reports from the table, stuffed them in a portfolio, and stormed out of the room.

The sales force, stunned by their manager's demonstration of wrath, for a moment seemed as statues cast in bronze. No one moved or spoke. After what seemed hours, but actually was only moments, one of the group rose to his feet. "You know, he's right. It's one thing to say what you're going to do, but it's another thing to do it. It is easy to make promises, but it is difficult to carry through—to deliver the goods."

Promises are oftentimes no more than cheap excuses offered in lieu of performance. Such promises are seldom worth more than the breath used to express them. They are but verbal dodges to escape the judgment of being weighed in the balances and found wanting. For this reason many people have developed a cynical outlook on promises of any kind, verbal or written. Promises between men and women at the altar are backed out of with the ease of backing a car out of a garage. Promises of politicians running for election are dumped with such frequency and regularity that many are making note of what is promised so they will know what won't be attempted.

Promises of both the great and the small ring empty and hollow. Contracts are breached, payments are ignored, and the fabric of man's whole society is strained to the breaking point. Promises without intent are not only immoral, they are the termites in the underpinning of what holds up our entire societal structure. No society can long endure the lack of confidence in its leaders, institutions, and the word of common, everyday folk.

If ever there were a time for a revival of basic integrity, a time for men keeping their word, and carrying through on their promises, it is now. Of course, there are times when circumstances are such that the best-laid plans of men go awry, but such are exceptions and not the rule. Men usually are able to do the things they want to do. As a rule, promises are broken, not because of outside circumstances which render them impossible, but because of the promiser's self-centered interest. When promises become expensive, inconvenient, no longer to one's personal interest, they are broken, regardless of the cost, interest, or inconvenience to the other party.

There was a time when a man's word was his bond. He would rather die than be found a person whose word was worthless. There are still men of such integrity. They are few and far between, but there are some whose word can be trusted. The world needs more of them, strong-hearted men of their word, men who can be trusted to move mountains, if necessary, to do what they promise.

Keeping one's promises is to become godlike. Faithfulness is one of the attributes of God. Faithfulness, reliability, trustworthiness—whatever its name—is the glue that holds society together. Our civilization, personal integrity, and eternal salvation depend on faithfulness to promises made.

Ditto Van Winkle

The Lord is at hand.   *–Philippians 4:5*

His name was Ditto—Ditto Van Winkle. Unlike old Rip Van Winkle, Ditto had not been alseep for twenty years. He might as well have been, though, because one day he woke up to what was going on around him. He had been so busy here and there with this and that, he just hadn't noticed how few people really cared about anything.

"Hey," he shouted to a passerby, "did you see what I just saw?"

"What did you see?" asked the passerby.

"That guy over there just beat on and stomped that little fellow into the gutter, and took his watch and wallet," explained Ditto, pointing to the attacker.

"So? What else is new?" shrugged the passerby.

"What else is new?" screamed Ditto. "Wouldn't you say that was a bit unusual?"

The passerby shrugged again. "Everybody ought to be allowed to do his own thing," he commented. Then he calmly passed by on the other side.

Ditto was frantic. He pushed through the passing crowd, whose faces were blank and expressionless. He summoned a policeman.

"Officer, officer!" he called. "Do something. That man walking off over there just clubbed, kicked, and robbed that poor fellow, and left him bleeding on the sidewalk!"

The officer looked at Ditto quietly and asked, "And what, Sir, would you have me to do?"

"Arrest him!" Ditto ordered.

"I'm afraid, Sir, that is quite impossible."

"Impossible!" Ditto repeated, incredulously. "Why?"

"Well, you see," the policeman explained, "that would be an infringement on the man's freedom to do what he likes."

"Freedom!" Ditto yelled back. "What about *his* freedom? You mean one man has the right to club and kick another man down, rob him of his possessions, and leave him bleeding and helpless in the streets?"

The policeman laughed from the belly and asked Ditto Van Winkle where he had been for the past twenty years. Seeing that he was getting nowhere with the law, Ditto hailed a cab and started to lift the injured man into the back seat while the cabbie watched.

"Look, fellow," the cabbie said, "if that guy is bleeding, don't put him in my hack."

"But this man is injured," Ditto protested. "He may die if we don't get him some help!"

"So?" the cabbie countered. "Let him kick off in somebody else's hack, not mine."

Looking around frantically, Ditto Van Winkle spotted a man of the cloth. "Reverend, Sir!" he called. "This man is injured. Will you help me?"

The clergyman looked on, then shook his head. "I'm sorry," he said. "I would like to help, but I have an appointment in ten minutes, and I am late already."

"In the name of God, man, what appointment could be more important than saving a man's life?" Ditto persisted. The clergyman looked for a moment as though he really wanted to help, but then he thought better of it. Instead, he made a theological observation: "You aren't saved by doing good, you know."

In desperation, Ditto looked up at the policeman, the cabbie, the clergyman, and the attacker. Attracted by the shouting, the attacker had come back to see what the commotion was all about.

Ditto pleaded, "If you have no compassion, then in deceny's name, will someone help me get this poor injured man to a doctor?"

At the mention of the word "doctor," each on-looker began griping over rising costs, loudly criticizing everyone in authority, mocking and cursing God and whoever else came to mind. In the meantime, the expressionless crowd went their several ways, to the X-rated movies and their own little sexual orgies.

Ditto Van Winkle threw up his hands in disbelief. "Doesn't anybody care anymore?" he cried out. The crowd, the cabbie, the policeman, the clergyman, and the attacker thought for a minute and then answered in chorus, "No, we *don't* care anymore."

And then a strange thing happened: the end of the world!

A Helping Hand

The righteous considereth the cause of the poor: but the wicked regardeth not to know it.   –Proverbs 29:7

Oftentimes, poverty is looked upon as the just dessert of one's own folly. The Bible says, "For the drunkard and the glutton shall come to poverty: and drowsiness shall clothe a man with rags" (Proverbs 23:21). Another passage laments, "He that followeth after vain persons shall have poverty" (Proverbs 28:19). Still, all poverty is *not* the result of indolence, riotous living, nor following after empty people and their soap bubble dreams.

A great deal of poverty is traceable to long and expensive illnesses, death, loss of employment, lack of opportunity, or the oppression of unscrupulous profiteers who crush the needy and grind in the faces of the weak. Such poor folk are victims of conditions not of their own making.

Solomon observed and wrote, "The righteous considereth the cause of the poor: but the wicked regardeth not to know it" (Proverbs 29:7). The question that keeps rising to the surface of my mind in the light of this Scripture is, where do we Christians stand on this important issue? With the righteous? With the wicked? One considers the cause of the poor, the other couldn't care less. Righteousness and wickedness in this particular matter have nothing to do with what one believes or disbelieves, but rather how one cares or does not care. This caring and not caring about the cause of hungry, naked, thirsty, sick, lonely, and imprisoned people, was also made a point in Jesus' teaching as being the difference between sheep and goats (Matthew 25:31-46).

Looking at the Word, I see definite needs. First,

let the Christian who sees a brother made poor by illness, loss of work, etc., reach out with a helping hand. The Master says, "Inasmuch as ye have done it unto one of the least of these my brethren, ye have done it unto me" (Matthew 25:40). Second, let the Christian who sees people made poor by indolence, riotous living, etc., take them the good news of the gospel. It is the power of God unto salvation up, over, and out of poverty. Third, let the Christian who sees people made poor by oppressors give warning to those oppressors: "He that oppresseth the poor to increase his riches, . . . shall surely come to want" (Proverbs 22:16).

Poverty is real, rough, and debasing, and God is concerned for the poor. Those made poor by oppressors He shall surely avenge. He expects His children to offer a helping hand to those made poor by circumstances. To those made poor by their own hand, He has sent the good news of His saving grace.

He Promised Too Much

Now we exhort you, brethren, ... be patient toward all men. —1 Thessalonians 5:14

I've just been sitting in one of those "instant" print shops, waiting for some printing that was promised, first for yesterday, then "first thing in the morning." Rather than run up and down the highway anymore, I elected to wait. The old saying is true, "The hinge that squeaks gets the oil." I just stayed in the shop and squeaked; as a result, I got my printing.

Let's face it; the world is full of people unable to deliver everything they promise. Most of them sincerely intend to do what they promise. For them and for us, failure to deliver the goods is probably due to biting off more than can be chewed. It happens not only to printers but to contractors, plumbers, repairmen, and preachers. Preachers too? Yes, especially preachers.

When people do not deliver the goods as promised, the big temptation is to trade one offender off for another. As I made the second long trip to the printer, my inclination was to trade him off for another. As I thought on this, some questions came up: What will the new one be like? Will his work be as clean and attractive? Will he be as personable and friendly? Will he be more prompt in keeping his promises? Those are unknown qualities. Maybe, I thought, what we need is patient firmness in encouraging and helping those who serve to establish realistic goals.

Some elder-friends were talking to me recently about their minister's failure to make calls, as they thought he should. They asked what they could do. Two options seem available to those men. They can trade off their offending preacher for another who may or may not be any better, or they can encourage the one they have to establish some realistic goals, and help him to meet them.

My printer would not have been helped by my trading him off. When we established a new goal and I waited for it, the work was done. It took some investment on my part, but all that time wasn't wasted. I entered into someone else's frustration of not having enough time to do all he had promised. I saw myself in his spot, and suffered with him.

The work finished, the printer apologized for having caused me to make that extra trip and to wait.

"I hope you will come back," he said, expressing half a hope and half a query.

"I will," I assured him. I am sure that the next time he promises me something, he will really try to be more realistic in setting his goals.

Isn't this just like most of us? We are all cut out with the same cookie cutter, called human nature. Our patience with each other is one way to improve relationships, and it is certainly a way of being more godlike. God is patient! His disciples should manifest the same quality. Patience is a Christian virtue, a fruit of the Spirit.

Stick-to-it-iveness

Be ye also patient; stablish your hearts: for the coming of the Lord draweth nigh. —James 5:8

During a session with my seminary students recently, we talked about a group-growth session, in which each participant was asked to draw a picture showing where he envisioned himself to be, spiritually. One participant drew a picture of an airplane on the way up, but showing someone parachuting out. Explaining her picture, the artist said that there were times in the ascent she felt like bailing out. This is not an uncommon feeling. We all have smiled at such statements as "Stop the world, I want to get off." A later one, referring to the Comet Kohoutek moving away from the earth at 200,000 miles an hour, commented, "Wise, very wise."

Sometimes we all feel it would be a good idea to pull out, jump off, or bail out! Asked if he ever thought of leaving the ministry, a friend of mine answered, "Yes, every Monday." Fortunately for himself and the good people he serves, my friend has been able to overcome this Monday temptation.

The Christian walk is a discipline. It is hard to buckle down to the commitment the Lord expects. Stick-to-it-iveness is a virtue, but it is in constant conflict with the flesh. Like water, the fleshly is always seeking its lowest level.

With the world as it is, with all of its pressing problems of increased crime and corruption in high places, one may think the Comet Kohoutek is quite wise in pulling away from the earth. With the mounting shortages of such simple human activities as courtesy and respect, one would want to stop the world and get off. It is even conceivable that with the responsibility of being Christian in our marriage, work, and recreation, one would want to bail out, to quit, to leap into the line of least resistance! But—we all know that kind of cop-out is exactly what is wrong in the world today. Too many have bailed out, stepped off, and pulled out.

Now, it may be hard to hang on to faith when all those about you are losing theirs. It may be hard to keep on trying when those around you have quit. But crowns are not worn by quitters, nor are victories won by those who throw down their arms and run.

The book of Revelation says the victorious ones, those who remain steadfast to the end, are the ones who:

Will be given the right to eat from the tree of life (2:7).

Cannot suffer the slightest hurt from the second death (2:11).

Will receive the hidden manna (2:17).

Will be given authority and the morning star (2:28).

Will wear white garments, and his name will be forever inscribed in the book of life (3:5).

Will become pillars in the temple of God (3:12).

Will sit beside Christ on His throne (3:21).

I Only, Am Left

For it is God which worketh in you both to will and to do of his good pleasure. —Philippians 2:13

In my experience as a church member, I have run into a lot of brethren very much like the young poet who had just sold his first verses. He was showing signs of deep depression, prompting a friend to ask, "What on earth is the matter with you? You have sold your first poems, yet you look so hopeless."

The young poet heaved a long sigh and replied, "Shakespeare is dead. Keats, Shelley, Byron—all are dead. The responsibility on my shoulders is almost more than I can bear."

Isn't it true that our spiritual depression often follows hard on the heels of some spiritual triumph? With God's help we overcome a besetting sin, or through His power we suddenly realize we are getting through in our prayer life. In our study we discover a profound new insight from the Word, or in our concern we help someone else through a spiritual crisis. Then it happens—we start feeling the awesome responsibility of having to live up to our new self. Suddenly the whole load is ours. Like Elijah, one gets to thinking he is the only one left who hasn't bowed his knees to Baal. That, of course, is reason to believe that if the faith "once and for all delivered" is to survive, he alone will have to save it.

It is true that many of the old saints of God are dead, and it seems there are not many people in the world who are interested in discovering insight from the Word. Few are interested in becoming prayer warriors, overcoming sin, or lending a helping hand. Still, there are some Christians left who are interested, who intend to contend for the faith and live for Jesus Christ.

God has not left us alone! There are many folk who are just as faithful, just as sincere, and just as committed as we are. Let us not be depressed, brethren! Let us rejoice that God has given us a part in the great scheme of redemption. He has given others a part in that same divine plan! Not one of us is Savior of the world. There is but one, and He has already come. We are only witnesses of the Savior. Let us stop our worrying and fretting over our Christian responsibilities and rejoice in being Christian.

Like the young poet, we sometimes take our responsibilities so seriously we lose the joy of the experience. When we lose the joy of being, we lose the very thing that attracts others to desire what we Christians have.

The Greatest Force

For God so loved the world, that he gave his only begotten Son. —John 3:16

Out of World War II comes the story of a Londoner's eyewitness account of the Nazi bombing of England's capital. Watching the explosions and raging fires that swept the city, the old resident said, "It seemed all was lost—the war, England, the values of our civilization. As I saw the docks and the center of London all burning, I wept like a child. But then a gust of wind cleared the smoke for a moment, and in that moment I saw the cross of Christ still standing on the dome of St. Paul's Church." Seeing that cross, the witness was comforted and stopped crying. He went on to say that in that moment of vision he knew there was "a power stronger than the swastika," a power that would carry them through, and London would live on.

It is true that the "worst" may appear the stronger at times, but Christ's cross reminds us that the "best" is greater than the "worst." No matter what power may appear, or what strength they may muster, there are some things that will abide. Among these are faith, hope, and love, and the greatest of these is love.

The Londoner's vision of St. Paul's cross was a reminder of our Christ's triumph. Touched with this heavenly power he was able to survive the fires of Hell itself. Though his beloved city was bathed in flame, this man knew that truth and high purpose could not perish in flames. Some things are indestructible. Heaven and earth may pass away, but God's Word will remain.

All of us are tempted at times to think all is lost. We see the blackened ruins of doubt, the raging flames of hate, the billowing smoke of despair, and we want to cry. But then, in a strong gust of the Spirit, we see the cross of Christ and are reminded that there is a power stronger than Satan, a power that will carry us through. Come what may, Christ's people will live on.

Don't let the times pull you down, for the "best" is greater than the "worst." Truth and high purpose are not defeated, not as long as there is faith, hope, and love; for faith is greater than doubt, hope is greater than despair, and love is the greatest of all.

Respecting the Lord's Day

It is required in stewards, that a man be found faithful.
–1 Corinthians 4:2

Someone has rightly observed, "Christianity begins where religion ends—with the resurrection." The resurrection of Christ took place on a first day of that week of weeks. As a result of that one historical event, every first day of every week has been regarded as "The Lord's Day." For years it was revered by the people of this country as a day for worship and rest. Businesses were closed. Factories shut down. People went to church, visited with relatives, rested, and reordered their lives for the week ahead.

That was before the secularization of our culture. Things are different now. Factories go full force, profit takers are open for the hoards of people who converge on their shopping centers to buy and trade. It is a terrible loss, this accelerated stampede away from anything sacred. It is all so frightening! Frightening, because as man ceases to believe in God he also ceases to believe in man.

Haven't you noticed? As men lose faith in the things they used to hold sacred, with the loss they become more selfish, greedy, immoral, and cruel. As reverence decreases, crime increases. As men lose faith in divinity they lose faith in humanity. With the increased disregard for God and His Word, we can expect more crime and less regard for basic human rights. When people lose respect for the Lord's Day, not far behind is the loss of respect for Him who gave the day significance. When men no longer believe in God, neither will they believe in him who is created in the image of God.

Easter marks the beginning of all Lord's Days. It

was on a first day that Christ arose from the dead. It was with that day hope was kindled in the breast of men. May we pray that the flame will not be extinguished by our lack of respect to the Lord or His day.

I am convinced that if the Christians would respect the day of the Lord they repute to serve, then the profit takers would find Sunday merchandising a most unprofitable pursuit and would again close their doors. A secular world understands loss of profit, even if it doesn't understand respect for the Lord's Day.

Communicating

Let all bitterness, and wrath, and anger, and clamour, and evil speaking, be put away from you, with all malice.
                                                    –Ephesians 4:31

Expelled from his homeland, Russia's most famous son, Alexander Solzhenitsyn, has made an observation that causes one to shudder in thinking of both the truth of his observation and the consequences of the situation he has observed. In his book, *The Gulag Archipelago,* he writes, "Violence is brazenly and victoriously striding across the whole world. There was a time when violence was a means of last resort. Now it is a method of communication."

The truth of these words is all too evident. Violence, tragically, is the modern man's major means of communicating with one another. It doesn't seem to matter who is communicating with whom—government with government, race with race, management with labor—the rule seems to be, "Clobber thy neighbor before he clobbereth thee." Worse, "Blow off thy neighbor's head in order to get his attention!"

Genesis 6:11 speaks of a time when the earth was filled with violence. God said to Noah, "The end of all flesh is come before me; for the earth is filled with violence through them; and, behold, I will destroy them with the earth."

If violence once caused God to repent that He had made man, what do you suppose He thinks about the present scene where men bomb, shoot, and burn each other as a means of communicating? If violence was the reason for the flood, it is reasonable to assume that violence could be the reason for the big fire that will surely come.

The Reformers?

The law is not made for a righteous man, but for the lawless.   *–1 Timothy 1:9*

I have no idea where the following parable originated. It has caught my attention twice, once when I clipped it, and again at this writing. The story goes like this:

Three reformers met under a bramble bush and agreed that the world must be changed.

"We must abolish property," said the first.

"We must abolish marriage," said the second.

"We must abolish God," said the third.

"Economic freedom is the objective," said the first.

"Sexual freedom is the objective," said the second.

"Freedom from religion is the objective," said the third.

"The first step," said the first, "is to reduce society to a common level."

"The first step," said the second, "is to cast off restraints."

"The first step," said the third, "is to eliminate the Bible."

"We will begin," said the first, "by abolishing rights."

"Let us begin," said the second, "by abolishing laws."

"The way to begin," said the third, "is to abolish mankind."

The parable is not as farfetched as it first seems. The truth is, the world's new trinity is the atheist, the libertine, and the Marxist. Through history these "reformers" have failed miserably in bringing one scrap of security or freedom to a single society.

It is unbelievable that they would still have an audience willing to give their schemes a listening ear. But, eerie as it may seem, there are those in this country who are not only listening to these self-styled "experts," but are even espousing such God-denying, Red-baiting, licentious theories as "solutions" to America's problems.

For a long time I have been alarmed about what has been written, and who is being quoted as having the answers. But surely the all-time low has been reached in a recent Sunday article in which a "lifer" was interviewed in a five-page spread as to what was needed in prison reform. Before I had finished the second page of that article, my heart was bleeding for all the poor inmates in our country's prisons, who were being subjected to all that cruel and inhuman punishment for such minor offenses as torturing innocent people to death, child molesting, cutting down peace officers, cheating the elderly out of their life's savings, gang raping of young girls, and purposely making dope freaks out of thousands and thousands of our young people. The interviewed "reformer," as I suspected, had a solution: "get rid of punishment." I was surprised that he wasn't as "with it" as some of his more educated peers, writing recently for a "professional journal." Their solution was, "Get rid of laws."

You have to admit, if there were no laws against murder, rape, robbery, and dope-peddling, certainly none of these things would be a crime. Do away with the laws and, presto, you've done away with crime. The question no one seems to bother to ask is, "If we get rid of the laws against murder, rape, robbery, etc., will all the murders, rapes, and robberies then cease?"

Well, not exactly. In fact, there actually was a time when there were no laws. During that time, the

Bible says, man became so corrupt that the earth was "filled with violence." There was so much violence that it repented God that He had ever created the earth. God put a stop to that first godless, lawless, and classless (they were all one low class) society. He washed the earth of them and started all over again. After that, He gave man some laws and some punishments as a consequence for breaking those laws.

Happily, there were some ideals worth stretching up for. When mankind's "experts" have been those who revere and respect those laws, things have gone well for man. But when mankind's "experts" have been the God-haters, libertines, and class-baiters, the result is a real bummer.

Who has your ear?

Forgetting the Image

See then that ye walk circumspectly, not as fools, but as wise, redeeming the time, because the days are evil.
–Ephesians 5:15, 16

A dress-making factory, which employed women, greatly reduced the rate of accidents on its company stairways. Despite warning signs, bright lights, and even monitors, the girls continued to fall while going up and down the stairs. When in a flash of genius the management mounted full-length mirrors on the stairway landings, the accident rate dropped to almost zero. Now the girls tend to walk with much more deliberation as they pass their own reflections.

One can't help but wonder how much more deliberately all of us would walk if we could see ourselves at each landing in life. I am sure a lot of the young would be less slovenly, if there were some way for them to see a reflection of themselves as they appear to others—their teachers, prospective employers, and especially to the Creator, who gave them bodies to honor, minds to stretch, and an eternal spirit to dress and keep. Many men and women who seem bent on appearing ''with it'' might be less ''common'' if they could catch a glimpse of how their everyday speech and behavior looks to Him who expects excellence in those whom He created in His image.

What would happen if some Christians we know would come face to face with a full-view mirror reflection of how far they have drifted away from their high calling? Such might be a sobering experience, in more ways than one. If strategically located full-length mirrors worked to reduce stairway accidents for the girls in the dress factory, one may reason that a few well-placed mirrors should also reduce the falls of men.

Well, before we rush out and buy some full-length mirrors, we might consider the fact that we do have a lot of mirrors in place. Our art, literature, and drama are all reflections of our culture, but no one seems to be paying much attention to the reflection. Our culture grows more slovenly, steadily sinks to a tawdry level, and drifts continually farther away from God and His truth. Movies seem to be getting dirtier and more violent, and art appears more distorted and confused, while religion makes fewer demands and disciples. Man seems to be able to see his reflection and straightway forget what manner of man he is. In the forgetting he just continues on as he was—unmoved and unrepentant.

Wouldn't it be great if mankind were more like the girls of the dress factory and upon seeing their reflections in the mirrors they would walk more deliberately? I guess some would classify the girls' more deliberate walk as vanity, but I figure anything that saves men or women from falling on their faces is not vanity at all, but just being smart.

Forgiveness Week

*Let us therefore come boldly unto the throne of grace, that
we may obtain mercy, and find grace to help in time of
need.* —Hebrews 4:16

With an estimated thirty thousand of their two-
million volumes overdue, the Free Library of
Philadelphia decided to proclaim its first "Forgiveness Week" for overdue books. The borrowers, delighted with the opportunity to return their delinquent books without having to pay the penalties,
returned 42,261 books.

I wonder if the church could declare a "Forgiveness Week" for its delinquent members. It would
work pretty much the same way as the Philadelphia
library plan. On the given week, all delinquent
members could come back to church fully forgiven
of all the pledges they didn't pay, all the promises
they didn't keep, and all the responsibilities they
failed to meet.

I think a "Forgiveness Week" would have a lot
going for it. I am sure that most folk do not mean to
shirk their responsibilities, or break their promises,
or rob God of what is rightfully His. Instead they just
got themselves deeper in debt than they should,
promised more than they could deliver, and probably thought more of their rights than their responsibilities. When folk get to thinking about their
rights, how overworked they are, and how much in
debt they are, they can justify all kinds of shirking.
Yet, though man justifies it all, somehow he never
can feel really good about it. Maybe it's the haunt-
ing memory of that passage of Scripture that keeps
saying, "But he that doeth wrong shall receive for
the wrong which he hath done: and there is no
respect of persons" (Colossians 3:25).

Let us have a "Forgiveness Week" when the penalties are forgiven. Those who haven't paid up will be forgiven. Those who have not lived up to their promises to God will be forgiven. Those who have not measured up to their responsibilities will be forgiven, all with no questions asked. Just bring in the life, or what is left of it, commit it again to the work wherein it was called, and start all over with a clean bill. Come to think of it, I guess that's what each Lord's Day is, isn't it, a kind of "Forgiveness Week" where delinquents can be forgiven and can start all over again?

Determining Priority

Seek ye first the kingdom of God, and his righteousness; and all these things shall be added unto you.

—Matthew 6:33

A key figure in the development of western Europe's medieval civilization was Carolus Magnus, better known as Charlemagne. By his military campaigns, Charlemagne created a vast empire in the west, which lasted in one form or another for more than a thousand years.

About the time our country was being born a republic, Charlemagne's tomb was opened for repairs. The sight the workmen saw was startling! There in the tomb, sitting on a throne, was the old conqueror, clothed in the most elaborate of kingly garments and holding a scepter in his bony hand. On his knee lay a New Testament, with a cold, lifeless finger of the other hand pointing to Mark 8:36: "For what shall it profit a man, if he shall gain the whole world, and lose his own soul?"

It is interesting to speculate how such a thing came about. Was it planned by Charlemagne himself before his death? Hardly! Was it a touch added by his kinsmen or advisors? Unlikely! Was it the act of some ordinary fellow who smuggled in a New Testament on the day of burial, and, in a pretense of a final adjusting of the kingly apparel, set the Bible and finger in place to be sealed forever? Probably!

Although such is interesting to contemplate, it might be more profitable for us to consider our own life's priorities. Charlemagne's priorities were to fashion an empire, and he did. He fashioned one that included all of the old western empire of Rome, plus much that was new. It lasted a long time, almost a thousand years after his death. But as it was with him, it, too, came to an end. Both he and his empire are gone, but the truth of that passage on his knee lives on. What will it profit a man to gain the whole world and, in the process, lose his own soul? Possessions and places, here and now, are small stuff, compared to the destiny of one's eternal soul. The place and possessions are soon taken over by another, and the soul goes to its eternal home. Whether that soul is saved or lost depends on what one's priorities were on earth. It all boils down to putting first things first.

Charlemagne's Latin name was Charles the Great (Carolus Magnus), but the least of all in God's kingdom is greater than the old empire builder known as "The Great."

The Character Generator

Blessed are they that hear the word of God, and keep it.
–Luke 11:28

Having been invited to be a panelist on a TV religious talk show, I met with three other ministers at the studio to pre-tape the program. While discussing what responsibility each was to take, we were told by the program director that he was ready for us to begin. Speaking to the host minister, the director apologized for the station's "character generator" being out of order. Not knowing what a "character generator" was, I thought, "What a shame! WTTV owns some kind of instrument that generates character, and it's broken!"

If ever there were a time America needed a "character generator," it's now. Just think what could be accomplished in government alone if we had a "character generator," generating a little character among our politicians. One ex-governor wouldn't be reporting in to begin a three-year jail sentence. One southern senator wouldn't be under a grand jury indictment, and all those careers of men connected with the Watergate mess would not be lying in smoking ruin.

No one can imagine how disappointed I was to learn that a "character generator" was not what I had imagined it to be. From the program director I learned that a character generator was an instrument to project a person's name on the television screen while the person is talking. The word "character" means the characters in the English alphabet, rather an individual's character.

Oh, well, it was too much to hope for anyway. How could there be an instrument that could generate moral strength, self-discipline, and strong constitution in the lives of weak human beings? Or is it too much to hope for? Come to think of it, I believe our society has a "character generator." The Bible, old as it is, is still in good working condition. The problem is that in our day and time the Bible is not used much to generate character. Modern man has cranked up some so-called new generators to generate character, but so far they haven't produced too much of the stuff of which character is made. More people are educated in the arts and sciences than ever, but there's less self-discipline. More people are affluent, but there is less moral strength. More people are free, but, for some unexplained reason, there is less true freedom. Freedom, wealth, and education haven't generated much character. All three promise a lot, but somehow they do not live up to their promises.

There is a character generator that actually does generate character, however, and that is God's Truth. Would to God that we as a people would use it again as such. I predict that we would see a dramatic change for the better! There would be better homes, better schools, better communities, better government. You know why? Because men and women of character just build better homes, schools, communities, and governments.

The Rising Cost of Trash

Through covetousness shall they with feigned words make merchandise of you. —2 Peter 2:3

The value of trash is at a record level. "One man's junk is another man's treasure." This was never more true than today. Old newspapers that once sold for eighteen dollars a ton now fetch fifty-five a ton. Some grades of scrap iron that brought fifty dollars a ton yesterday bring $160 a ton today. Scrap copper has doubled in the past year, and such common items as bottles and tin cans bring twenty dollars a ton.

It all sounds like a fantastic price that the recycling people are willing to pay for trash, but it pales in comparison with the millions, yea, billions of dollars that Americans are paying for a different kind of trash. Let me explain. Right now there are some people who spend all their time and energy looking for written trash that majors in violence and sex. This trash is not worth the paper it is written on. These people will pay fantastic prices for the "scum rights," and then spend equally fantastic sums to produce their perverted flicks. Why? Because they realize what profit can be made on the rising value of trash. With a few more dollars spent on clever advertising, they resell their garbage to a trash-consuming public. The take is unbelievably high, amounting to billions weekly. A triple-header of trash billed as "Don't Look in the Basement," "Last House on the Left," and "Mark of the Devil" had cars in Indianapolis lined out into the highway.

There are two kinds of trash dealers. There are the respectable ones who contribute to a cleaner environment by buying old papers, bottles, and cans. Then there are the unscrupulous ones who buy up "litter-ary" trash and recycle it into trashy visuals to clutter up the minds of thousands.

The optimistic prophets keep predicting that the day of trashy movies is ending, but the facts fail to bear them out. Movies are not getting better, but worse, and they will continue to get worse as long as trashy films are profitable. When sex and violence are no longer profitable, then and only then will such films end.

You know, if those who call themselves Christians would stop buying trash, I am convinced that the margin of profit for trash films would be so clobbered that the whole industry might do something positive about getting out of the trash business. As long as it is profitable for the film trash dealers, you can expect more trash films. Of course, the high cost of trash films is not measured in dollars and cents, but in the corrupting influence they have on the minds of our people. The increase of crime and perversion is partly traceable to the filmed junk that comes to us at such a high price.

Self-acceptance

There is therefore now no condemnation to them which are in Christ Jesus. —Romans 8:1

Sydney Harris points out that Abe Lincoln was one of the few politicians who knew how to turn back an accusation with humor. Once, when reproached by an opponent for being "two-faced," Lincoln screwed up his homely countenance and replied good-naturedly, "Does anyone imagine that if I had two faces I would choose to wear this one all the time?"

The opponent had to be squelched. Who, upon hearing such a reply, could resist siding with the President? I imagine that even the accuser himself was amused at the quick wit of the country lawyer from Illinois.

Being a Lincoln buff, I am always amazed at Lincoln's complete acceptance of himself. Surely one of his greatest talents, as a human being and as a leader of men, was that he knew who he was. In this knowledge he accepted himself, warts and all.

Self-knowledge and self-acceptance are an important combination for victorious living. A lot of people have accepted themselves without knowing who they are. On the other hand, there are a lot of people who know who they are, but cannot accept themselves. It is a human tragedy to be trapped in either situation.

Let us consider first that person who has accepted himself but doesn't know who he is. The real danger is that such a person is all too willing to accept his weaknesses as limitations that cannot be changed. Unmindful of a man's potential as a son of God, these folk plod along in life on a sub-level of behavior, excusing it all as their being human. The great truth of the Scriptures is that God has called us to a vocation above the natural state of being just creatures. God has called us to be sons and daughters (2 Corinthians 6:18); to partake of the divine nature (2 Peter 1:4); to enter the everlasting kingdom (v. 11). If one does not know this, he is unaware of his potential and then makes no effort to live above the natural state.

Let us consider next the person who knows he is a child of God but cannot accept himself. He sees himself in contrast to the sinless one and cries out, "Woe is me, for I am undone." Of course, there is nothing wrong with our seeing our iniquity and sin, but we must also see how Christ has taken away our iniquity and purged our sin. As believers we are washed in the blood and are made right through Christ's righteousness.

If we could only accept ourselves as saved by the power of Christ, and see ourselves as sons of God through faith, I am sure we would be much less defensive in our relationship with each other. We might even demonstrate a little humor in those times when our accusers charge us with hypocrisy and inconsistency.